start right
start big

an action guide for building a prosperous business

by Charlene Schuster Knox & Angela E. Soper

For all those who believe they deserve
a life filled with prosperity and happiness
and are willing to take action
to make their dreams more powerful
than their fears.

Contents

From the Authors

People write books for many reasons. Most nonfiction authors would say they write books because they have knowledge to share with others. We created this book as an offshoot of a similar book we wrote for the direct selling industry—an industry we know well since combined we have over 35 years of experience working in a variety of capacities related to direct selling and network marketing.

We realized that many of the action steps we talked about in our book for those involved in a direct selling venture apply equally well to *any* kind of business a person may be starting or already building. And that's why we decided to revamp this material so anyone who considers himself or herself an entrepreneur can use it to put some tried and true—and quite often simple—action steps to work for them so profits go up and anxiety goes down.

If you think about it, business is business and some elements bridge the gap between the different kinds of businesses that are out there. It really doesn't matter if you're selling tires in a store, African jewelry via the Internet or you are a personal trainer to the stars—you still need to be able to communicate effectively with potential customers, get your name before the public, come up with innovative promotions, speak and write well, find techniques that will keep you motivated and headed toward your goal, and create collaborations with other business owners that will generate a win-win situation for everyone involved. And that's just a few of the ways business needs are often similar.

We invite you to cruise through this little book with an open mind and a good dollop of enthusiasm. If you are guided by your vision and are committed to building a successful business, this book can help you fine-tune your efforts and solve some of the dilemmas you may encounter on your journey. You've undertaken the hardest part: making the decision to follow your bliss. Now it's time to shore up that decision with some easy-to-do action steps that will give you an edge in the marketplace.

We don't profess to have all the solutions and we certainly can't guarantee your success in the endeavor you have chosen. However, we do know that those who *do* succeed are focused on their goal, are driven to reach that goal, and are not afraid to be bold and daring when the occasion calls for nothing less.

Now turn the page and start reading, then keep this book handy to combat moments of confusion, doubt or panic. And remember ... if you truly believe in yourself and your idea, you can often overcome any obstacle that may be lurking in the shadows.

Thanks for letting us be part of your "action plan" and please let us know if some of the actions you learn about in this book prove helpful to you.

Here's to your success ...

Charlene and Angela

Preface

The Right to Fulfill Your Dreams.

If you've picked this book up in a store or clicked on the "Look Inside!" tab on a Web site, you're probably someone who is really serious about creating a highly successful business and who enjoys learning new ways to improve your life—personally as well as professionally. For that, we offer heartfelt applause. We hope this small book will become another valuable tool in your learning process and that you'll uncover some true gems in these pages that will help you create the business *and the life* you envision.

First of all, we want to make it clear that the ideas presented in this book aren't "brand new" and "cutting edge." That's because there are no original ideas in this universe; we can't think of anything that hasn't been written about, spoken about or tried in some form by someone else. But … old ideas are often reshaped to give them new appeal and innovative twists that offer people a better chance at succeeding.

Go into any bookstore, and you will find dozens of books about how to be successful. You will find new titles designed to help you master the law of attraction—a concept that has been around for many, many years. There are books out there promising to solve your weight loss woes, your dating frustrations, your frazzled parenting angst and even books that offer new techniques for adding red-hot sizzle to your sex life. And you know what? We, the authors, have bought a lot of those books (we aren't telling which ones, though). That's because we enjoy finding new ways to tackle an old problem or rethinking some aspect of our lives we feel needs improvement.

And that brings us to this book, *Start RIGHT. Start BIG. An Action Guide for Building a Prosperous Business.* We created this book with one simple goal—to give you some easy-to-understand and easy-to-do actions that will help you build a business you enjoy *and* will start giving you the lucrative financial rewards you want.

And that, beauteous ones, brings us to our next point: desiring wealth. If you have ever thought it was wrong to desire wealth, we ask that you put that notion out of your head right now. Go ahead, stew about it for a few minutes and then pluck it from your brain and give it a good hard toss so it lands far, far away from your mental stratosphere. *There is nothing wrong with wanting to be wealthy.* But we don't mean you should desire Gordon Gekko's brand of greed, either. Gekko is the character played by Michael Douglas in the 1987 movie *Wall Street*. In the movie, Gekko makes it clear he believes greed is good. *Really* good.

Greed and desiring wealth are two separate, very distinct desires.

And that leads us to a little book that is a real treasure when it comes to aligning your vision with your potential. *The Science of Getting Rich* was first published in 1910 by Wallace D. Wattles and was reportedly the inspiration for the best-selling book and film, The Secret by Rhonda Byrne. While *The Secret of Getting Rich* offers terrific advice throughout its pages, what we really like about the book is chapter one: "The Right to Be Rich." Here Wattles explains that it is impossible for people to realize their potential if they're living in poverty. He says: "No man can rise to his greatest possible height in talent or soul development unless he has plenty of money; for, to unfold the soul and to develop talent he must have many things to use; and he cannot have these things unless he has money to buy them with."

Wattles made this statement because he believed people develop in mind, soul and body by making use of things. He goes on to say that society is organized in such a way that people must have money in order to become the possessor of such things. He makes it clear in the book that people should have all that they need in order to experience the power, elegance, beauty and richness of life. "To be content with less is sinful," he says.

Okay, now you're probably trying to figure out why this theory is different from good old Gordon Gekko's "greed is good" mentality. Wattles equates wealth with having the ability to enjoy life to its fullest. This means having good food, shelter, comfortable clothing, freedom from "excess toil" and enjoying rest and recreation. Also included is the ability to travel, to read and study, to surround oneself with art and beauty, and to love because "love is denied expression by poverty." Wattles is saying (we believe) that wealth is a good thing when it is used to help individuals enjoy life and *not* that a person should desire wealth merely to possess everything that is available, or that individuals should aspire to be rich simply for the sake of being rich.

Finally, Wattles highlights this right to be rich with a simple yet profound belief that people find the highest happiness by bestowing benefits on those they love. "Love finds its most natural and spontaneous expression in giving."

And this, to us, is really the gist of what Wattles tried to get across to readers in 1910, and the point we feel needs to be made today. It's okay to be successful—to own the car of your dreams, to buy a nicer house, to take your family to Europe, to wear attractive clothing, and to retire when you're still in good health without having the burden of working until you're 70 just to survive. It's what you *do* with your wealth—*and how you obtain that wealth*—that matters.

If you build your business with integrity and along the way are focused on helping others achieve their dreams, you deserve to be rich. If you use your wealth to make the world a better place, you deserve to be rich. If you are grateful for the success that you achieve and if you give back to others throughout your journey, you deserve to be rich. If you are kind, honest and sincere and always take the high road when faced with challenges, you deserve to be rich.

We hope this little book will help inspire you to set your goals high. We want you to have the success you desire and deserve. Each action offered in the following chapters is designed to propel you

---

forward and upward. This is a book you can keep handy and refer to often. It contains tried and proven techniques that can help you get organized, become a better communicator, create new prospect lists, and even get yourself unstuck when success appears to be eluding you.

This isn't a get rich quick book. Trust us; you won't make your millions right away. But it is full of ideas that can lay the groundwork for building a very rewarding venture. And we believe if you put some of these actions into motion today, you will be one of the people who is truly making a difference in the world and who is proving dear Mr. Wattles correct: "There is nothing wrong in wanting to be rich."

Chapter 1

Prosperity Starts With Vision.

Prosperity starts with intention, vision and usually calls for something to change in your life. Why? Because a dream is stirring. You can feel it. It's a yearning for achievement—something that you can see for yourself. In fact, if you close your eyes, it's there in Technicolor. It may not yet be crystal clear, but chances are your soul is telling you: "Decide that you want it!" "That you intend to have it!" and "Start taking action!"

To sum it up simply, your heart and soul are telling you to determine—*and act on*—your compelling vision.

Your compelling vision can be anything so long as it is important to you. Maybe it's a vacation house in Italy, the sports car you've longed to own since getting your driver's license at 16, sending your children to a top university, or creating a hefty nest egg for retirement that will ensure your financial security. Whatever it is, find a picture that represents it or write it down, and keep it clearly in sight so you're always reminded of your compelling vision, day in and day out.

Rarely do your dreams come true all at once and none just happen through magic. The desire to change something in your life and go for your dream often comes when you have some kind of big wake-up call. Like losing your job, getting a divorce, a loss of a parent—all bridges in your life that millions of people have to cross every year—like it or not.

If you want to make a change and make that dream yours, one of the world's most recognizable marketing phrases comes into play: Just do it! Make the decision. Make the commitment. Learn what you have to do … and just do it. It's easy to analyze too much. To compile lists and visit therapists for answers. You ponder endlessly: "Why am

I afraid?" "What are the positives and negatives?" Eventually, you may end up so confused and frightened about making a change that—as our own grandmothers may have said—you've scared the tar out of yourself. At some point you just have to make a firm decision to "go for it."

If you dream of being wealthy, then don't let anyone tell you that dream isn't practical or realistic. There's always a way to change things in your life so you can reap the many opportunities for wealth that are laid before you. To help you clarify your vision, answer these questions: What do you love? What makes you happy? What are you doing when hours turn into seconds? If you're living an "okay" life but miserable because of the work you're doing, then you're squandering your passion and talent. And such squandering, dear one, is not okay.

An opportunity is out there that aligns with your dream and can provide a way to improved wealth as long as you are willing to make the journey, potholes be damned. Avoid thinking about failure and why things won't work out. Be positive. Believe in you. Stand up for what you deserve and fully embrace the idea that you have the right to live an abundant life.

Claim the life of your dreams and do something—anything— but move closer to your compelling vision with relentless conviction. Remember that prosperity follows passion. Now get passionate and get going!

Action: Grab a pen and paper so you can begin to articulate your vision. Use adjectives to paint the picture through words. Then, find the pictures that represent that vision. Create a vision board on an 8″ x 10″ canvas using words and pictures. Place it on your desk so you realize that every day your efforts are moving you closer to your dreams.

Chapter 2

Finding the Right Opportunity for You.

If you're reading this book, you obviously have a business or desire to start a business. In the course of the next chapters, we'll guide you to specific actions that will help to increase your results and therefore your success. But, just in case you have not settled on exactly what kind of business you want, we encourage you think about all the possibilities before you.

Opportunity is defined as a set of circumstances providing a chance or possibility for a stroke of good fortune—good fortune that can either be grasped or lost. Opportunities are all around us. There are possibilities everywhere waiting to be discovered and capitalized on; oftentimes they come when we are trying to solve our own problems.

Take Edward Lowe. Back in the 40s he invented a clay formula that soaked up grease and oil. One day a neighbor asked Edward for some of his clay to help housebreak her cat. It wasn't long before Ed knew he was on to something. On to something indeed. Edward Lowe went on to supply 40 percent of a $400 million litter box market.

In 1948 Gene Autry was looking for a Christmas song that matched his first hit, "Here Comes Santa Claus." A New York songwriter mailed Autry a recording of "Rudolph, the Red Nosed Reindeer." Autry did not like the song and had no intention of recording it. However, his wife would not stop pestering him because she thought their kids would like the song. At the very last minute Autry recorded what he thought was just a silly, simple song. Need we say more? Hundreds of millions of copies of that song have been sold around the world and is the most recognized holiday song on the planet.

You may not be looking for things like cat litter and hit songs, but be sure about this: There is no limit to the opportunities before you. There are so many out there waiting to be discovered by people like you who are determined to act upon them. The question is: Will you be bold enough to take action or will you let someone else run with it? Don't wait another day to claim yours!

Action: Be sure you have selected the right opportunity that fits your passion and purpose.

Chapter 3

The Power Behind a Personal Sound Bite.

The first words out of your mouth can make or break how well you impress someone. Sorry, no stuttering, hem-hawing or vagueness allowed. It's critical that you create and polish your own personal sound bite so you have a succinct, memorable, defining statement that explains who you are and what you do. If you want to promote your business and increase your earning power, you simply must have a killer sound bite, dahhhling.

That's because in today's world of always-ringing cell phones, on-the-spot texting, and multitasking you have no time for a novel. Even a novella is too long. We're talking synopsis, baby. Short, sweet and to the point. This is your commercial jingle and you want to "Wow!" everyone who hears it.

In 10 to 15 seconds your sound bite must explain:

1. Who you are

2. What you do

3. Why you make a difference

To help you hone your memorable spiel, use these seven steps:

1. Write the first thoughts that come to mind that answer the questions: Who are you? What do you do? How do you make a difference? Circle each descriptive word you've written. Then list each descriptive word to the side of the paper. Next, place the listed words in the order of importance.

---

2. Draft a sound bite of two or three sentences. Give prominence to the most important words on your list. Don't sacrifice clarity for cleverness. In fact, avoid humor.

3. Read your sound bite several times and trust your ear. If you trip over certain words, just change the words. Remember to showcase the most important points first.

4. Underline key words you want to emphasize. Recite it again and again until you are comfortable—until you believe it with total conviction. If you don't believe it, no one else will either.

5. Time how long it takes you to deliver your sound bite. It must be 30 seconds or less. Don't memorize it—instead, envision the key words.

6. Practice your sound bite in front of a mirror. Concentrate on looking sincere and confident. Stick with it until your presentation is smooth and powerful.

7. Then practice, practice, practice on people—friends, family members, unsuspecting strangers on the street (just kidding about that one). Imagine you're before your ideal customer/client each time you present it.

The most important thing is to trust your instincts. You'll quickly learn how and when to alter your message for your audience. Already have a sound bite? Make sure it's updated and powerful by completing steps one through three.

Here's an example of a powerful sound bite:

"What do you do?"

"I teach women how to achieve a higher level of earning power."

"Really?"

"Yes."

"How do you do that?"

"I have developed a coaching system that allows women to master sales, people, marketing and life in all aspects of their business. I help them learn how to think, what to do, when to do it and why they're doing it. It's all about how to wildly succeed in life and gain the prosperity everyone deserves. Here's my card if you'd like to know more. I have a free introductory class on Tuesday evening at nine. If I may have your contact information, I'll send you the details."

Action: Create a personal 30-second sound bite promoting you and/or your product or service. Practice. Practice. Practice.

Use this space to write your personal sound bite.

Chapter 4

A New Twist on Finding New Business.

It's a fact of life: Stumbling blocks happen. So, don't despair, dear heart—we are here to help you smash through that dastardly wall of frustration and emerge on the other side like the confident, enthusiastic person you are. It's time to expand your business by expanding your contacts. Get creative and create a list of people who will want your product or service, and even include those who may consider joining your business if you're looking for business partners.

Imagine it's your tenth anniversary and your business has gone to million-dollar heights. That's right; you're earning more money than you ever thought possible. Today, you've decided to throw a big thank-you party—Bruce Springsteen will be your headliner, and money is no object. In fact, rumor has it George Clooney will make an appearance. Can you feel your heart fluttering?

Okay, okay … time to get back to business and an important question: Who would you invite to such a magnificent event? Wouldn't you want everyone you know to come and enjoy the celebration? Of course you would! So get out a piece of paper and start *that* list. Because this is the event of a lifetime, you wouldn't want to leave anyone out. When you're finished with friends, family, associates and business partners, move on to people you *don't* know, but *want* to know! In a matter of 30 minutes you could have a prospect list with an easy 500 names.

This idea works for any kind of business. If you're in retail, you will want to hold a "grand opening" event to introduce people to your merchandise. If your business is strictly an Internet venture, you will want to make sure everyone knows about your new business and the site. If you are offering a service, like personal coaching, again you will want people to know what you offer, why you offer it and how they can become a client.

Once you have assembled your list of names, prioritize the names, fill in the rest of the contact information and start contacting everyone. Shouldn't you be just as excited about your new business as for your anniversary party? The only way to get a million is to remember all of the people who may be interested in what you are selling.

Now, take a deep breath, limber up those fingers, and start inviting!

Action: Use your millionaire mindset and create a contact list of everyone you know (and don't know) who can help you launch it big!

Chapter 5

Creating Your Very Own Work Space.

This chapter is primarily for people who work from home or at least do the bulk of their day-to-day business (like bookkeeping, product ordering and marketing) at home. If that's the case, you need to define *your work area* as such, circle the wagons around it and protect it with all you've got. Intruders will encroach on your space at every opportunity—even the little ones you love with all your heart—and you may soon find yourself spending more time keeping work-related items organized than you do on building your business. And that's not good.

First, make it clear to everyone in your family—even the dog who sticks beside you like glue—that your work area is your work area, and no one is allowed to rearrange papers or folders, plop sticky popsicle sticks down on your writing surface, or fiddle with your computer. If the dog insists on barking every time you make a phone call, learn to be the alpha dog and assert your authority (seriously—dogs can be as manipulating as 2-year-old children!). If you have to share your computer with other members of the family, carve out a specific period of time when that is allowed. If possible, buy your own computer and make it "hands off" to everyone else (we recommend a laptop since they're so portable and if things get really bad, you can always take a laptop into the bathroom with you and lock the door—no kidding, you think we haven't done it?).

If you have the luxury of using an entire room as your office, decorate it so it is your haven. If you want to repaint, think about the color and how it will make you feel. Blue represents peace and tranquility and reportedly can slow the pulse rate. Green represents nature, good luck, healing and calmness. Orange expresses energy; purple royalty, transformation and wisdom. And yellow is joy and optimism.

If you can, add a sofa or an easy chair so when you need to "think," you have a comfortable place to do it. Lighting is crucial—both good light for seeing but also light that adds a soothing ambience. Pink light bulbs are great for softening a room (they'll also make you look better when you glance in the mirror). Don't forget aromatherapy—here again certain scents can have different effects, so investigate the fragrances that are available.

Add touches that are important to you. Maybe it's a quote that has always inspired you—try stenciling it on the wall or have a friend who is good at calligraphy write it for you. Put up pictures you like. Maybe they're pictures that represent your compelling vision or places that simply make you feel good—like a gorgeous Caribbean beach. Have a way to file important information, a nice desk with a big surface area, and use baskets or bins to keep everything organized. For heaven's sake don't clutter your area, that will only add negativity to your life.

If your work area is a corner of the living room or kitchen, schedule your work time when others in the house aren't at home. Or, get up early and do your work before the chaos begins. If you like the quiet and solitude of late night, try to do paperwork when the children have gone to bed. If you need to make important calls when the children are home, make it clear that you are not to be disturbed. A prospective client or customer does not want to hear a child wailing in the background, and the distraction will make it impossible for you to think clearly and listen well. If your toddler and the dog are both bent on sabotaging your efforts to get something done, find a teenager who will babysit for an hour or two and take them outside to play.

Sometimes it makes sense to obtain an office outside the home. You might consider partnering with a friend who would like a similar part-time arrangement. Maybe she could have the office mornings, and you could have it afternoons. An office outside the home (talk to your accountant about tax deductions for home offices) is a tax-deductible expense, so it may be a worthwhile investment. If not now, maybe as your business grows.

If you're serious about building a business, then you must make it clear to everyone close to you that your work is a serious venture and they must respect the time you need to devote to it. And if you set up your boundaries in the beginning, they'll be easier to maintain as you gain more success and get busier.

Action: Claim and organize your personal work space.

Use this space to create a list of necessary office equipment and supplies.

Chapter 6

Adjust Your Money Mentality.

Creating a "money mojo" mentality helps you attract the income you want. If you think small, chances are your business will always be small. But if you start thinking about the large income your business is bringing you, chances are also pretty good you'll start making more money.

First of all, imagine that every penny you spend is an investment in yourself. If you're throwing money away on items you don't need, adjust your spending habits and start investing in yourself and/or your actual business. Does that mean repainting your store so it is bright and welcoming? Perhaps you need to get a massage to help relieve anxiety. Maybe you need to invest in clever promotional material that will help "get the word out" about your new business venture. You may need to hire a really good Web designer who will turn your web site into an easy-to-navigate and innovative extension of your business goals, services and/or merchandise. And perhaps you need to take a class that will help you simplify your finances or use new computer software to enhance your record keeping.

Here's a fun exercise that can also help you attract the financial abundance you want. Imagine you have no limitations on the quantity of money you can attract and that you would use this money for the good of humanity. Next, think about the charitable organizations you feel most aligned with and that you would enjoy supporting. And finally, take action! Find a cause that is close to your heart and donate something—anything—even if it's only $10. Giving to others comes back to you, and the more you give, the greater your rewards. Try it— it works!

Now, what are your human resources looking like these days? This means your gratitude, your sense of style, your sense of humor and your compassion. Are you rich in these areas or lacking a little bit? If you find yourself always thinking negatively, check yourself the next time a negative thought comes to mind. When this happens to us we immediately recognize it for the damaging thought it is and tell it to get lost. Then we come up with a positive thought about the same subject. The more you are aware of how you're thinking, the easier it is to correct bad habits.

Do you fuss and fret over every little problem? If so, start looking for the humor in situations or remember that common adage: Don't sweat the small stuff. Do you feel like the world is against you because you don't have the wealth of someone else? Take a close look at what you do have and start counting your blessings. Remember, there will always be people who have more material wealth than you. And there will always be people who would love to be in your shoes.

Action: Put the following sentence on a small card and repeat it every day: "Everything I need for an abundant and prosperous life is available to me." Make sure you display the card in a place where you will see it every day.

Chapter 7

Identify and Share What You Love.

You may be excited about everything connected to your new business venture, but chances are there is something that really *rings* your bell more than anything else. Identify what that is and use it as your springboard for sharing your story and your business with others.

Whatever your product or service is, there is probably one benefit that resonates with you more than others. Capitalize on that love and use it to draw people in with your own personal testimony. How did this product, service or your business change your life? What one or two benefits solved a need in your life? Say it with passion and crisp articulation.

Here's an example of how you can tell people why you feel so passionately about your product/business/service:

"I started my own business so I would have the security, freedom and flexibility so many of us desire. In my business, I bring products and ideas to people that help them improve their overall well-being and enjoy life more. Maintaining a healthy mind and body allows us the energy to accomplish what we want to get done on a daily basis. So why settle for anything less? So now I'm helping others and also achieving my own goals, like working around my family's schedule instead of an employer's demands. Don't believe it when they say 'You can't have it all'—having it all *is* possible!"

People respond to personal testimonials. That's why you see them every time you turn on the television and find an infomercial. How many times have you been tempted to buy a product because the person on the screen told you *it really worked for her?*

We can't vouch for the honesty of infomercials, but we do know testimonials sell. And if you have a personal testimonial about your product or service and are passionate about what it has done for you, you will attract interested people. Lead with passion and follow through with your integrity and you are bound to capture an audience—and that's half the battle right there!

Action: Create a powerful testimonial about your product or service that can help you influence others to support your business.

Chapter 8

Present with Perfection.

You have a vision and belief of what your product, service or business can do to help others or solve a need they may have. You will obviously speak tirelessly and relentlessly to make people aware of what you offer.

Presenting your offering is not about "telling" people what to think and feel about it, it's about "shaping" how they will think and feel when they have heard your presentation. Project your passion and vision into the hearts of your listener. Breathe life into your delivery. Be compelling and concise.

Next, think of support tools that may help you present your offering. Is it a quick video from a flip camera on your Web site that can help you create a powerful presentation? Do you need an unusual business card, maybe in the shape of a bookmark? What about a printed card in an interesting size that you can leave behind so people will be aware of your business and know how to contact you (an odd size or bright colors stand out from the standard size business cards most people hand out). Don't go overboard with lots of printed pieces and expensive tools. Settle on one or two ways to get the message out.

Remember—this is a fast-paced world and people don't have time (or *think* they don't have time) for long, detailed pitches. Be creative and be succinct and make it easy for them to contact you and learn more. If you can provide samples of your product, that's a great way to entice people to purchase your product (this is especially important when you are participating in festivals or events where vendors rent space to sell their merchandise).

We're reminded of a woman who was selling homemade fudge at a small town festival. No one stopped at her table. Why? Probably because she had no samples out for people to try. And any candy lover knows that one taste of irresistible fudge is enough to prompt a sale on the spot. A few dollars spent on providing samples could have meant a *lot of dollars* in sales by the end of the day.

If your business is a service that is primarily Internet-driven, you may be able to provide a sample of your service that people can download for free. For example, if you are marketing a service that helps people create powerful résumés, you could offer a "Ten Worst Mistakes to Make in Crafting a Résumé" download for people that would educate them and perhaps encourage them to use your skills. Not only would the download give them valuable information, it could also contain testimonials from satisfied clients.

There are lots of ways to attract attention and pique people's interest about your product or service. Know your target audience, know the best-selling benefits of your product or service, and get out there and present … with perfection!

Action: Create a presentation plan that will bring desired results. And never leave home without your business information and support tools.

Chapter 9

Meld Your Passion into Your Business Plan.

Most of us have a cause that is close to our hearts. For you it may be helping to stop child abuse, creating a green environment in your community, supporting breast cancer research, or saving an endangered species. If you can find a way to support your favorite cause as you build your business, you may find that your day-to-day efforts become more exciting and more meaningful. That's because the more success you have, the more you can benefit your cause and society as a whole.

There are several ways you can combine supporting a cause as you build your business. You can contribute a percentage of your income on a monthly, quarterly or annual basis or hold a special event that you and your business "sponsor," with all proceeds going to the cause. If your business involves selling products, you could give a portion of sales on selected items to your cause; or, you could donate products to a charitable organization.

Your product itself may have a natural tie-in to a cause or partner. For example, if your business involves selling products that support women's well-being, you may want to partner with a local health clinic that promotes the benefits of everyday wellness and routine checkups. Together you could hold a Women's Wellness event and as part of the service for those attending, you could offer mini facials or hand massages using your products to demonstrate the value of pampering one's self. You could also create a gift basket that would be given away to one of the people attending.

If you sell a service, like designing Web sites, you could team up with a charitable organization and help design its site, then offer to give a percentage of any new business received for a certain period of time to that organization. You would be identified as the designer for the organization's site with a link to your site and the special promotion you are offering.

The important thing is to build your specific interest into your business plan right from the beginning. Your initial contribution may be small at first, but as your business grows you'll be able to be more generous—and that's a great feeling!

Action: Identify a cause that matches your passion and begin to support it immediately as you launch your business.

Chapter 10

A Great Bio Brings Big Business.

In addition to having a great résumé that you keep up-to-date, you must also have a short bio. Why? Because there are times when a bio is all people want to see. This is especially true when it comes to speaking engagements, or when you're interviewed for a magazine or newspaper article. A bio covers the highlights of your career and life in just a few sentences. It provides the reader the essence of you and what makes you so darned fantastic.

A great place to see samples of good bios is on the back cover of a book jacket. Read a bunch of them to get a good feel for what makes them compelling and then work on crafting your own. It's usually harder to write a short message than a long one, but keep at it until you feel you've captured "you" succinctly and well. Make sure it is grammatically correct and there are no punctuation errors. Have someone read it to see if it captures the best aspects of your professional accomplishments.

You may also want to write two or three versions of different lengths. You'll discover that some people want a 50-word bio and some may want a 200-word bio. So be prepared. If you write a magazine article, the editor may want just one or two short sentences that identify you. And if it's an article about a certain topic, you may want your bio to relate to the subject; for example, you're writing about a recent special event you hosted to benefit homeless pets. Your bio might include a line like: Successful entrepreneur Jane Doe has been an animal lover since childhood and usually conducts teleconferences with her rescued beagle snoring at her feet.

Here's a sample of a well-written, 49-word bio:

Jane Doe is the CEO and founder of Lives of Dreams, a nonprofit dedicated to helping children fulfill their potential. She is a renowned public speaker, has started several successful companies and is a contributing editor for *The Power of the Feminine* magazine. Learn more about her at *www.anywhere.com.*

Action: Write your own "book bio"—you never know when the press may call or when you may have a book in you just waiting to be written.

Chapter 11

Define Your Unique Story.

Everyone has a unique story. You've probably heard that old adage, "Be you, everyone else is taken." Well, it's the same when it comes to launching and promoting a business. Those who focus on their "story" have a much better shot at creating compelling marketing materials. That's because people like to hear how ideas were formed, why someone has such passion for her product or service, the history behind the business, the different personalities that make up a business, or the intriguing circumstances that resulted in the product or service you offer.

Patagonia is a case in point. Its founder, Yvon Chouinard, didn't set out to create stores and a sportswear line known around the world. He just wanted to make climbing gear he knew would make his passion for climbing more enjoyable and easier. He began by creating a black-smith shop so he could make his climbing hardware. Soon other climbers wanted the equipment. Then he started designing and creating better outdoor wear. Again, people wanted what he was making. Today Patagonia is known for its social and corporate responsibility, its flexible work schedule for employees, and its commitment to pre-serving the environment as well as for its high quality merchandise.

If you're reading these words and racking your brain trying to figure out what about you or your business could possibly be interesting, take a deep breath, exhale and get a pen and pad of paper. We're going to walk you through a quick exercise that will help you identify your unique story.

1. Make a list of everything about you. This includes where and when you were born; who your parents are/were; number of siblings and your placement within the sibling hierarchy; your dreams as a child; your struggles as a child; your fond memories

of childhood; your education from elementary school to your highest degree; the activities that bring you joy; the activities you dislike; your job history and what you liked and didn't like about each job; your experiences as an adult—your marriage, children, hobbies, etc. Include the heartbreaks of your life as well as the events that have brought you immense joy. Also include people in your life who generate positive energy, as well as those who tend to pull you down with negative energy. This will help you both avoid those who may be detrimental to your vision and surround yourself with those who are beneficial to your business.

Don't worry about form or structure—just write and get it all down. Spew from your heart and mind. And yes, you can use a computer if you don't like writing by hand. As you start thinking and remembering, you will find that you will uncover memories you had forgotten about. You may even get a little jarred and emotional, and that is perfectly okay. Sometimes it is the deep stuff that is the most motivating.

2. Once you have completed this list, go through it and start highlighting the events, actions or dreams that have stuck with you through the years. Is there something from your past that has remained locked away in your heart and is the impetus for the business you have created? Was there a situation, action or personal need that helped you create the product or service you are now selling?

As you go through this exercise you may find that your past and everything that makes up your personal history is what makes you so unique. It's what drives you today, or makes you determined to be successful. Tragedies may have made you stronger. Moments of bliss may have reinforced your need to help others enjoy happier or more productive lives.

As you look at each situation you wrote down, especially if it revolved around actions you took or beliefs you held at the time, ask yourself why each of those experiences took place. Maybe you passed up an earlier opportunity because you were afraid of failure, and you now realize had you had the courage to grasp that opportunity you would have a better life today. Now you have a new opportunity and you don't intend to let it pass.

Those who search for buried treasure must dig. And dig some more. And dig yet more. And that's what you must do now. Dig into your past and into your hopes and dreams and life experiences and find a way to capture that "story" that defines who you are. You will find the treasure that defines you and that will help you market yourself and your business more effectively and passionately.

Action: Create your list of life experiences and start developing your unique story.

Use this space to begin to develop your personal story.

Chapter 12

Put Your Best Face Forward.

First of all, like it or not, people often like to see who they're dealing with. You won't always need a photograph of yourself, but when you do, by gum you want it to be absolutely fabulous, darling. And we mean fabulous. So, that means you don't hold your cell phone up in front of you and snap a shot, and you don't ask your friend who doesn't know one end of a camera from another to take a photo of you.

People who coach online dating clients always recommend that those seeking love online invest in having high quality photographs taken. And that's because a good photographer knows how to make you look your best. That doesn't mean you need someone to touch up your photographs (as they do in the upscale magazine world when a company is selling a beauty product). It just means you are dressed, made up and positioned in the most flattering way possible. You will also want the photographer to take *a lot* of photos. Professional photographers do this for magazine covers and then editors sort through them all to find the "one" they feel will capture the most attention and sell the most magazines.

Remember that in addition to selling your product or service, you are selling *you. Always, always you are selling you.* Think about the stores you no longer patronize because the help is surly or the owner is about as helpful as a tree stump. People should be impressed by how you look, how you talk and how much you know. And if you believe you never take a good photograph or you hate to have your photo taken, or you simply don't like how you look, get over it—please. It is your personality and passion for what you do that will convince people to do business with you. Or entice a television producer or magazine editor to feature you in a story. But they also don't want to see a slob or someone who looks exhausted. Trust us, not every successful entrepreneur looks like Brad Pitt or Angelina Jolie. If you're smiling and your eyes sparkle with energy, that's going to come across in the photo. If you're dressed well (something that is flattering—so no flowery moo-moos if you're overweight) and aren't sporting a questionable hair style (like a style that died in the fifties and should stay dead), you'll give an impression of competence.

Remember to update your photo from time to time. Just as people get annoyed when a person on an online dating site posts a photo that is 10 years old (we could tell you stories, but that's another book), your professional contacts won't appreciate a photo of you that is woefully outdated. Be proud of who you are and make sure your photo expresses that sentiment. Shop around and find a photographer who has taken great photographs of others. Show up for your shoot with two or three different outfits—you may at times want a really professional look and at other times you may want a more casual look, depending on how and where you'll use the photo.

Now, say "cheese," smile and put your best face forward because sometimes, pictures really *are* worth a thousand words.

Action: "Snap" to it and get a professional photo taken.

Chapter 13

The Magic of Networking.

Talk to successful business owners, and you will soon learn that they aren't shy about talking to people. That means they approach people they meet on a daily basis. And for many, maybe even you, that really places you outside your comfort zone.

However, there are few businesses that don't rely on "networking" for more frequent and bigger sales. Remember we told you earlier that when you speak from the heart with passion about your business and/or product, people are more apt to listen and be intrigued. We're reminded of a successful bread entrepreneur we know who makes grocery shopping more than just a necessary task; she turns it into true guerrilla marketing each time she spots shoppers browsing the freezers where her bread is stocked. She enthusiastically tells customers how good the bread is and touts its many benefits, but doesn't tell them it's *her* bread. Although her children refuse to go shopping with her (and if you have children, especially teenagers, you understand), she believes so passionately in the quality of her product that she has no intention of keeping quiet when she sees a prospective customer.

And that's the belief system you must possess to move your business forward. And it really doesn't make any difference what kind of business or service you're promoting: a caterer looking for people who could use your culinary skills, an artist looking for gallery venues, a personal fitness trainer looking for clients, or an inventor of a great new insect repellant looking for insect-bitten customers. Whatever it is, you must find people who want what you have to sell. And that means talking to people and finding out how you can solve a problem in their life or improve their life.

A good friend of ours is an artist who decided to use her talent to paint miniature portraits of people's pets. She had 4" x 4" cards made with photos and information about her custom acrylic portraits, and she hands them out when she sees dog and cat owners or is near a pet store. Even her friends (like us!) give out the cards when we're with a dog or cat lover or are in a store that caters to pet owners.

All of this means stretching your comfort zone and connecting with the people you encounter every day—even perfect strangers. If you're swooning at such an idea, grab your smelling salts and read on. It's really not as awful as it may seem.

As you develop your business you'll soon learn how you are most comfortable talking with people—especially people you don't know. And when you have your sound bite mastered so it rolls off your tongue as easily as your name, you're ready to connect. And just how do you connect? It's really pretty easy.

Just think about the people you routinely encounter. Like the people you're standing next to in the grocery checkout line. Or the other parents cheering on your child's soccer team. How about those people you smile and say hello to all the time at the gym? The interesting professionals you meet at cocktail parties, the woman walking her dog every day that you always pass and nod to, and the waitress you've gotten to know at your favorite coffee shop. And how many people have you sat next to on an airplane? Since most businesses and products are connected to a Web site these days, the world is truly your stage if your product or service can be marketed internationally.

You don't have to be a chatterbox—just friendly and genuinely interested in what they do. That means you should first listen and discover their interests and needs. Then if they ask questions about your business or product, you have a golden opportunity to tell them how much you love what you do, and you can tailor your response to match their needs. If you think about it, you'll realize there are dozens of people you encounter who might be interested in the product or service you offer. *But they won't find out about it unless you tell them about it.*

If you're still quivering in your Prada pumps about approaching strangers, start out with a few people you know just to build your confidence. Once you see that it's really more gain than pain, try approaching people you don't know and say, "May I give you my card? I'm starting a new business in the area and would love your feedback on my Web site." This is an easy, no pressure way to share information about your business with people you don't know.

Action: Learn the magic of networking by connecting with people every day. Make it part of your lifestyle and watch your business grow.

Use this space to list groups or events where you can master your networking skills.

Chapter 14

Walk the Talk.

A confident pace, a brazen strut, a stiff march, a casual stroll, a shuffle—they all paint a picture of the kind of person you are before you say your first word. Perfecting the way you walk can make or break your image. Your body language speaks a thousand words and even adds important punctuation and emoticons—like exclamation points, question marks and smiley and frowny faces. And it all starts with standing tall. A graceful, straight posture will give you a dignified appearance and add professionalism and elegance to that critical first impression. (Remember, you never get a second first impression.)

Great posture has many benefits, including the way your clothes hang on your body and helping you look more slender by appearing taller. All of this portrays confidence, self-assurance and grace. The right walk can take you places you have never been before—and we're not talking about cruising the new mall, honey.

If you have a dog, take her along with you for company. You can even practice your 30-second pitch on her or run new ideas by your faithful four-legged companion. (If she howls, you'll know you need to start over!) If you need motivation, see if a neighbor will join you on your daily walks. There's nothing like someone banging on your door to get you up and moving.

And, just to encourage you to get out there, here are a few wellness benefits of walking: A daily walk helps control your weight. Combined with healthy eating, adding a brisk walk to your life at least three times a week can help lower your blood pressure, decrease your risk of heart attack, boost good cholesterol, lower your risk of stroke, and just plain make you feel better inside and out. Walking is also a great way to clear your mind and focus on an issue at hand.

So go ahead—step into it and take a walk. You'll have everyone in the neighborhood commenting on your stature and poise, and you'll be strutting your stuff like the successful entrepreneur you were meant to be!

Action: Take a 10-minute walk—with or without a friend of any species.

Chapter 15

Listen More and Talk Less.

The little elephant Dumbo didn't realize how valuable his big ears were at first. But when he finally figured it out, life changed in a great way for him. And that's just what can happen for you if you remember how important your "big ears" can be—when you're talking to others. Here's a test: When you're on the phone, do you automatically start to doodle, put away dishes, check e-mails or maybe even watch television? You probably said yes. Well, starting today, commit to *listening* when you are on the phone. That's right, listen without multitasking. We know, we know ... that is soooooo old fashioned. But it's one of the secrets to connecting with people and learning how to solve their problems, and your business or product has the ability to change people's lives in positive ways, right?

Henry David Thoreau said, "It takes two to speak the truth— one to speak and one to hear." Studies show that over 80 percent of people admit to doing other activities while talking on the phone. Even though you probably pride yourself on accomplishing something while you're involved in a phone conversation, you're really sabotaging your chance to connect with the person on the other end of the line. And if that person is a potential client or customer, you may be missing sales and a promising relationship.

You've probably heard that you should smile while you're talking on the phone even though the other person can't see you. That's because what you're doing has a clever way of filtering through your entire system and emerging through ... you guessed it ... your vocal chords. So if you're distracted, the person you're talking to will sense it. And if she senses you're distracted and not paying attention to her (it's like looking elsewhere instead of into the person's eyes in a face-to-face conversation), she's not going to feel respected or important. And if she gets that feeling, she isn't going to be interested in getting involved with you or your product.

Did you know McDonald's "You deserve a break today" is the best jingle of all time according to *Advertising Age?* Well, it's because somebody listened in 1971 to all those calls from women who told the company about their daily routines. The idea to create a jingle using that theme originated from what McDonald's heard from those women. They listened and today billions of people throughout the world are taking a break and buying hamburgers.

"Excelling in selling" starts by listening to the people you speak with on the phone and in face-to-face situations. When you listen to others' needs you will quickly find solutions to help them enjoy life more. So go ahead—have big ears when talking to others—you may fly as high as Dumbo on your way to even greater success!

Action: Work to improve your listening skills. Call someone today and listen more, talk less.

Chapter 16

Find a Mentor. Be a Mentor.

Yeah, yeah … we know. You're too old for a mentor. That's for kids, right? Wrong, dear heart, wrong. We all need mentors because there are some pretty incredible teachers in this world. Your job is to find a person or maybe even several people who strike a real chord with you. Maybe it's someone in your industry who has overcome incredible obstacles to achieve even more incredible success. Or it could be someone who is a natural born leader and is the kind of person you hope to become. Then again, maybe your mentor is an author or someone you know about but have not nor will ever meet.

Whoever it is, learn all he or she can teach you. Think about the wonderful teachers you had in school who made you a better student or better person. This is the kind of person you want to study. Pick her brain, ask questions, take notes and most of all … *listen.* The beauty of learning all you can from a person you admire is that one of these days what you learn will be fodder for someone else. And one of the best tributes to achieving success is knowing that there are other people in this world who want to learn what you know.

So open your ears, eyes and heart and start listening and reading. Find the people who match your values and dreams and start learning.

P.S. And pleeeeeeassseee don't be afraid to change something you may be doing ineffectively. Or get your hackles up if you receive a little criticism. Just think of criticism as the stone polisher that is going to make you, a rough-cut diamond, absolutely dazzling and worth a fortune. Got that?

Now that you have been mentored, pay it forward. Be open to mentoring others and feel the joy in seeing someone succeed because you cared enough to share your knowledge and time.

Action: Find a mentor (whose values you share) for support and guidance.

Chapter 17

Like-Minded Allies Create a Win-Win.

As you begin to build your business and add contacts to your list of potential customers or clients, think about the people, companies and nonprofit organizations that would be ideal partners for promoting both of your businesses and causes. You can add links to each other's site and even offer small "advertisements" on your sites.

Special events are a great way to work with a partner. Perhaps you supply the man power and your partner provides the venue. For example, if your business is selling homemade organic soaps and lotions, you could create a special event at a local spa. The spa would use your products that you supply, and you would both promote the event. This is an ideal Mother's Day promotion or Mother-Daughter event. You could also donate part of the proceeds to a cause such as breast cancer research.

If your business is personal coaching, you could partner with a local women's shelter to help the women residing there learn ways to build their self-confidence and get their lives back on track. The ideas are endless, and all it takes is some thinking and finding the right partners. This is another reason why it is so important for you to constantly connect with people. By striking up conversations with others and letting them know what you do—and learning what *they do*—you may find an ideal partner for a special joint venture.

One of your goals with such events is to acquire new contacts who may be interested in the products or services you provide. That means creating a short survey form or asking people to fill out a form to be eligible for a prize drawing so you capture their names, phone numbers and e-mail addresses. Whatever you do, make sure you design a way to acquire the names and contact information for all those who attend the event. You can have a drawing and give the winner a product or perhaps a sample of the service you provide (e.g. a short personal coaching session).

Another advantage to co-sponsoring a special event is the publicity it may provide for you and your business. If you can also support a good cause as part of the event, you're likely to attract media attention, and that's a great way to promote you as a business person.

One of your jobs as an entrepreneur is to find innovative ways to market your business. And one of the best ways to promote who and what you are is to create win-win situations with companies or non-profits that share your passion. They're out there—so start looking!

Action: Find a new partner this week and create a winning event.

Chapter 18

Integrity Builds a Business That Lasts.

From the very start of your business venture, you must be a person of your word. You know how much you appreciate people who are on time, keep their commitments and treat you with respect and honesty. Well, that's the kind of person you need to be as you build your business.

Think about it, doesn't it really gall you when a friend—who is so wonderful in many ways—habitually shows up late? You are repeatedly tapping your toe waiting for her to arrive for a lunch date. Or you miss the beginning of the movie because she's late. Or she shows up an hour late to your dinner party and wonders why you started eating without her. To keep the friendship you probably grit your teeth and try to overlook this flaw of hers (because no one is perfect).

However, and this is a big however, when you're trying to sell products, acquire clients or work with an organization on a joint venture, arriving late is not only unprofessional—it's downright deadly business-wise. If you have a habit of being late, take steps right now to change. Leave the house 10 minutes earlier than you think you should. Set your watch 10 minutes ahead. Get up a half-hour earlier. Whatever it takes, *just do it!*

Being a person of your word also means keeping your commitments. The old saying, "under promise, over deliver" is a good rule to sear into your mind. If a product a customer wants is on back order, let the customer know when the shipment will arrive, and then make a point to call her when the product is in stock. If it is further delayed, let her know that also. If possible, give her a free product or coupon off a future purchase to make up for the delay (this means buying a few extra low cost items to keep on hand for such situations). If you promise to help with an event (e.g. a chamber of commerce function), make sure you perform the tasks asked of you.

And remember this: As you build your business and go through life, you're going to make mistakes. Sorry, but it's a given because mistakes happen to the best of us. When you make a mistake, own up to it. One of the best ways to lose friendships and mar your reputation is by constantly blaming others for something that went wrong. A sincere, "I'm sorry, I made a mistake," is far more gracious and forgivable than trying to point fingers at someone else. Learn from your mistakes and try not to repeat them. And don't beat yourself up over every little faux pas. Just move on and use this bump in your journey as a valuable learning tool.

And one more thing: Say thank-you, and mean it. Let others who are helping you know you appreciate their help. This goes for the grocery bagger who takes the time to carefully pack your produce so it won't be bruised as well as the corporate executive who takes the time to brainstorm with you. Just keep the following phrase (one of our favorites) in mind and you'll be a person of integrity: Be kind and honest . . . it matters.

Action: Values sell—so keep the bar high.

Chapter 19

Learn to Say Yes to No.

Day in, day out you're asked to do things by other people. Maybe it's your boss, or your children, your spouse or even a friend. And sometimes you're more than happy to help people. It's what makes you human and gets to the core of your compassionate spirit.

However ... and you need to pay attention here ... there is a benefit to saying yes to no. Why? Because your health depends on it. We're talking about your mental health, your physical health and your spiritual health. If you are always saying yes to everyone, you will quickly discover that you're saying no *to yourself* way too often. We call it getting the yes/no balance out of kilter. And if it's one thing you want harmonized in your life, it's your yes/no balance.

Women are notorious for caving in and saying yes when they really would rather say no. For example: It's raining and your son doesn't want to walk four blocks to school in the rain. Your husband is in a hurry to get to the office, he's going the other way, and he tells the kid to wear a raincoat, or carry an umbrella and start hoofing it. You, on the other hand, feel sorry for your sweet child and schlep into your raincoat and dutifully drive him to school. Then your best friend calls and pleads with you to go to a concert with her because her husband bailed. You don't really like Yanni (well for crying out loud, of course he bailed!) but you go to keep her happy. And then you get a call from a nonprofit organization asking you to please, please, please mail their solicitation envelopes to the people on your block. You sigh, cave in again, and tell them to sign you up. Sound familiar?

If so, then it's time you put some steel in that gorgeous backbone of yours and remember that it is okay to say no. Emphatically, unequivocally *no*. If you don't say no when you truly don't have time, don't have the interest or just feel someone is taking advantage of your generous spirit, you sap yourself of doing things for you, like pampering yourself for 20 minutes, or reading a book (like this one!) that will help further your professional goals, or writing in your journal, or taking a class, or maybe just spending quality time with your significant other.

Self-help professionals will tell you that spending your life serving others (without sufficiently taking care of your own needs) will drain you. And then you end up not doing a good job for anyone—including yourself! And just remember this bit of advice from the experts: In an emergency on an airplane, the instructions are to use the oxygen mask first before helping someone else. Got that? That can easily be translated into serving your own needs so you have the vitality and honest enthusiasm to be of service to others when you truly want to be.

Now, turn off the phone, put on some relaxing music, lie down for a few moments, and think about all the things you would like to do *just for you*. Then set a goal to do at least one of them before the week is out. And if you have to pass on the monster truck rally with your husband and sons (or if you're a man, the goofy chick flick with your wife and daughter), so be it. Remember, your health depends on it.

Action: Be courageous. Step up and say yes to no when you *know* it's best for you.

Chapter 20

Leverage Social Media to Grow Your Business.

Viral Marketing gets the word out about your business, but social media brings the world to your business. Two out of every three Internet users visit a Web site through some use of social media. Some of the social media leaders, including Facebook, Twitter, LinkedIn and YouTube, have drastically changed the way people connect with each other.

When utilizing social media, your job is not to hit people over the head with your product or service, but rather attract like-minded individuals into your community in an organic, business marketing way. As a business owner, it's important for you to communicate honestly and use all kinds of methods to share your story. There are many ways to connect with your audience, such as streaming video and audio, posting photographs, writing a daily or weekly blog or even posting short comments on a site like Twitter.

Twitter founders Evan Williams and Biz Stone knew that people were lacking time and getting frustrated with the status quo, so they decided to shake things up a bit. No more long content allowed. You have to say what you want to say in 140 characters or less. The result: People are flocking to Twitter like there is no tomorrow, selling ideas, books, products—all because they cleverly answer the question: "What are you doing?"

The Internet is an interesting communication tool. People who would not feel comfortable saying hello to strangers on the street are perfectly okay with inviting strangers who share the same interests to become part of their own online community, and encouraging others to look at their offerings.

Remember, it's a numbers game. Hundreds of millions of people are members of social media sites. Even if a small percentage like what you offer, you will reach more people a lot quicker than by word of mouth or one at a time. You never know who will become your next customer, so use social media and your ability to connect with people in your daily activities to grow your business.

Action: Select at least one social media site and set up your profile and story today!

Chapter 21

Write Well … It Matters.

It doesn't take a lot of time or study to develop good writing habits. For many people, a letter that is filled with poor grammar and incorrect punctuation is an immediate turn off. Buy a style book (many people go by rules in *The Associated Press Stylebook*, called the bible of the newspaper industry). Even people who make a living as writers use this or other style books frequently. If you feel really weak when it comes to expressing yourself in writing, take an English teacher to lunch and ask her or him for a few basic pointers. Show the person a letter you'd like to send to someone and have the expert go over it with you.

Another good idea is to take a writing course through your local community education program. These courses usually are inexpensive, and they offer a quick way to learn or relearn some good basic writing skills. And who doesn't need to brush up on dreaded dangling participles and the tragedy of split infinitives?

Because one of us is rather anal about certain writing mistakes that make her cringe, here are a couple of common mistakes you can easily learn to avoid: First, the period and the comma (or exclamation point or question mark) always go within the quotation marks. It's, "Learn the basics," she said. Not, "Learn the basics", she said. One of the best lessons on quotation marks came from one of our son's first grade teachers (bless her for teaching such youngsters the rights and wrongs of punctuation). She told the kids in her class that quotation marks are hoobie-doovers. And hoobie-doovers *always* go outside punctuation that is part of a sentence. We like to think of them as little secret service men and women who are protecting the president and his family. Cool, huh?

Another common error: putting an apostrophe in the word "its" when it is used as a pronoun. For people who know good punctuation, this mistake is especially annoying, and you don't want to annoy anyone, right? Just remember this simple rule: If you can't substitute with *it is* or *it has,* then you don't put an apostrophe in it. So: *It's* really quite simple to make this word fit *its* intended purpose.

You can also search the Internet for great grammar tips. Another book we love and use constantly is Patricia T. O'Conner's *Woe Is I—The Grammarphobe's Guide to Better English in Plain English.* Not only is it packed with great information, it's fun to read.

Now you know, so make sure you put those hoobie-doovers where they belong, okay?

Action: Find and enroll in a writing enrichment class in your community.

Chapter 22

Box Up Your Worries.

Here's an idea that psychologists and self-help gurus have been using for years: creating a personal worry box. It's a great idea for freeing yourself from all those worries, fears and anxieties that nag you night and day, and it's fun and simple to do. Imagine that—enjoying the fine angst of worrying!

Find a box around the house that has a lid and decorate it. Or, if you aren't the decorating type, just label it with a piece of duct tape that says: My Worry Box. Now take a few minutes and write on individual little sheets of paper everything you are worried about, and we do mean *everything*. Don't hold back! Concerned you gave your sister the wrong advice? Put it in there. Worried that your son won't get his science fair project finished in time? Write it down, stick it in the box. Afraid you won't find the right dress to wear to your friend's fancy birthday bash? Yep—write it down, and put it in the box.

Next, you're going to give yourself permission to worry 15 minutes out of every day. That's right; *you get to worry about everything* in this one block of time. How cool is that? For years, people have been telling you to "stop worrying about it!" and we're telling you it's okay—*worry about it!* But there's a catch.

Bring out your box and draw out your worries one at a time. Ponder each one—as many of them as you can for 15 minutes—then the ones you are still worried about go back in the box. The worries you have eliminated are thrown away. Did you give your sister the right advice? You're not sure you said the right thing when your sister asked you a life question that really mattered to her. Offer the best advice you can and don't worry if you said the right thing; people are smart enough to work out their own problems and you're smart enough to provide the right support. Your son's science project? If he

---

doesn't get it done and gets a bad grade he's learned a lesson about responsibility and consequences—and one bad grade isn't going to ruin his future. That perfect dress you're after? It's not what you wear but whether you enjoy yourself that matters, and anyway, it's only a few hours out of your entire life so why does it matter?

Fifteen minutes later, your unresolved worries are back in the box, and the box is on the shelf until tomorrow's worry time. Now you can get on with your creative and positive actions for the day because worrying is behind you. But don't worry—you'll have your 15 minutes to worry and wring your hands in despair tomorrow!

Action: Make your very own Worry Box today.

Chapter 23

Duct Tape Blues.

It happens to everyone—some days you just feel as if you are wrapped in duct tape and stuck to the floor. Your mind doesn't work, your body doesn't want to move, and all of those dreams and big ideas that were recently charging you like a 200-volt battery are simply languishing in a listless pool at the back of your head. You seem paralyzed with fear or are just flat out of ideas. We call it getting the Duct Tape Blues.

Well, for times like this you need to do a few things. First, take a deep breath and tell yourself this is only a momentary lull in your action plan. Then try some of these tactics to recharge yourself and rip off the mental duct tape that seems to be keeping you immobile—in body *and* spirit.

1. Write a list of 50 things that make you happy. Yes—just stop and list at least 50 things that will bring you unbelievable joy.

2. If you are getting too many "No's" on your sales calls, maybe today it's time to make a call to your best friend. Get some encouragement and catch up on the latest news and temporarily change the "Who" in your call and then see if the next calls you make don't bring you more positive results.

3. Take a nap. That's right—shove your to-do list under the pillow, and just sleep on everything for a while. If you can't sleep, just relax with some deep breaths and try a little power meditating. That means forgetting the stress in your life and focusing on the calm and beautiful of your life. You may want to invest in some meditation CDs to help learn how to soothe your soul and detangle your thoughts. At the very least, try playing calming music or listen to a CD that makes you toe-tapping happy.

4. Revisit your compelling vision. Take five minutes to think about why you want to achieve the goals you've set. If you need to find another picture or expand on your compelling vision, go ahead. The important thing is to make sure it's in sight every day. Even if you've already found a photo of your vision and posted it around the house, take the time to find new photos or write down a new list of its importance and replace your original pictures with these images or lists. Maybe you can even find a new place to post your vision that will help reinforce your efforts to reach your goals. Remember, the power of your compelling vision opens up your mind and new possibilities.

5. Make a big list of everything that's on your mind. And we mean everything—even the small stuff. Then enjoy the fun part—crossing off what really doesn't matter, or what you wait to worry about, or worry about when there is absolutely nothing you can do about it. You'll be surprised how few things that matter are left. And any worries left over go into your Worry Box. We know you'll always find something new to worry about (who doesn't?) and the trick is to keep tabs on those scoundrels and put them where they belong—gone!

Once you learn how to fight the Duct Tape Blues, these occasional lulls in your progress won't seem like such a downer.

Action: Pick an action from the list above to get unstuck and back on track.

Here's a little song you can sing as you get your attitude and energy realigned with your vision:

I got the duct tape blues

Oh, I got the duct tape blues

Feelin' so low, feelin' so bad

'Cause I got the duct tape blues.

Gonna kick 'em away

Gonna tell 'em to scram

I just ain't livin'

With duct tape blues.

Use this space to remind yourself what brings you joy.

Chapter 24

Become an Expert.

A great way to gain publicity about your business is to become an expert. This takes time, but you can start building your "expertise portfolio" immediately.

Let's take the example of a makeup artist. As an independent business owner, she/he needs to become an expert on makeup application, and the best type of makeup for the specific assignment at hand. If the person is an expert in fashion makeup and has a chance to do the makeup for a theater production, she or he may want to take a course on how to apply makeup for the theater.

The idea here is to become an expert in your field and use tactics like blogging entries to build up your credibility in this area. If you're participating in special events, find ways to submit articles about it to print publications that are open to receiving outside work. You can also query publications in your area with an idea for a story. Did your knowledge and/or products help a customer boost her confidence and ultimately help her get a new job? Have you perfected a quick and easy makeup system that women can use when they're in a rush? You may even be able to get a regular assignment writing for your local paper— a column devoted to a subject matter that relates to your product or service.

The important element is exposure—and we don't mean wearing a revealing top to the chamber of commerce luncheon. You want to put yourself "out there" as someone who can voice an opinion related to your business. The more your name and/or face are seen and your thoughts presented, the more credibility *and* publicity you and your business gain.

You'll soon find this becomes a win-win situation for you and those who seek you out for an opinion or advice. Why? Because the more you know, the more effective you'll be at selling your product or service.

So start learning all you can and soon you'll be looking in the mirror and seeing an accomplished expert staring back at you.

Action: Determine what five key things make you an expert in your particular business.

Chapter 25

Know and Use the Media.

Now really, some things are best left out of the paper and six o'clock news (like the morning you locked yourself out of the house wearing nothing but your pajamas and your daughter's shaggy dog slippers). But it is important that you let the world know what you're doing when it comes to your business. And if not the world, at least your community and regions where you hope to attract customers and business partners.

As your business grows, you'll want to promote events and specific successes you're experiencing. This means developing relationships with people in the media. Study the magazines, newspapers, and radio and television stations in your community and find out which reporters cover business news. Make a list and update it as personnel change. Whenever possible, send individual e-mails to media contacts. And learn how to attach a photo (which should be high resolution, usually 300 dpi). If you do send an e-mail to a group, be sure to bcc all recipients; it's very unprofessional to send out an e-mail that shows recipients all of the addressees. A press release should be one page in length—any longer and your pitch may get pitched—right in the trash bin. We've included a sample press release at the end of this chapter to use as a guide for creating and publicizing your own important news.

And remember to plan ahead if you want to receive coverage about an upcoming event. Find out the deadlines for each publication or broadcast station and note that in your file. And always, always try to find a creative way to pitch your story. Editors don't want to hear the same old story, and you shouldn't be telling it, either. For example: Did a recent accomplishment enable you to help out a worthy cause in the area? Are you introducing a new product with unique ingredients that are backed by amazing clinical trials? Or maybe the ingredients are all organic and come from local suppliers. Have you created a clever new way to make holiday giving easier? Are you donating products to a philanthropic organization?

When you do get a call from a reporter, be prepared to answer his or her questions succinctly and well. Your sound bite may come in handy here. Rehearse supplying a reporter with information about that particular story and give him or her short, snappy answers. If the reporter has to wade through a rambling monologue, you may find yourself missing from the day's news. And that, my dear, you do not want.

Action: Take a giant step. Write a press release for your new business and send it to local media outlets.

Sample Press Release

FOR IMMEDIATE RELEASE

Contact: [Your name]
[Email address and phone number]

LOCAL ARTIST TO TRANSFORM CHILDREN INTO IMAGINATIVE ANIMALS
Jane Doe Will Turn Playwright's Fantasy Musical Into Whimsical Characters

[Your City, State] – [Date for releasing information] The Magnificent Children's Theater Workshop announced today that local artist and makeup expert Jane Doe will transform local children into the wild and outrageously wonderful characters created by playwright Ima Doozey in his widely acclaimed musical, *When the Barnyard Came to Life.*

"When Joan Black, the director of this delightful musical, called me about doing the makeup and costumes for the production, I was thrilled," says Doe. "This has been a favorite story of my family's for years. Working on it will be a real treat."

Doe will create over a dozen costumes and makeup looks for the wide cast of characters that include a wise-cracking duck, a sleepy pig, two snooty horses, a confused cow, three yodeling sheep, four gossipy hens and a neurotic dog. "I've worked with Jane on several productions, and I knew she had the imagination to turn these kids into really fun characters," says Black. "The audience is going to be laughing from the moment Farmer Ben walks onto the stage with his crazy dog Ralph."

Doe is well known for her makeup work for film, television and print productions around the country. She is also one of the head costume designers for the Tri-State region's annual charity gala, The Masquerade Ball, held every November.

When the Barnyard Came to Life opens Thursday, September 23 and runs through Sunday, November 7 at The Magnificent Children's Theater Workshop located at [address], downtown [city]. Performances will be held Tuesday through Saturday evenings at 8 p.m. with matinees Saturdays and Sundays at 2 p.m. For ticket information, call [Phone number] or visit the theater Web site, [Link].

Chapter 26

May I quote you on that?

How often do you read the back of a book and see who endorsed the book and what they had to say? Probably anytime you pick up a book to see if you want to read it, right? Research says most people do. In fact, prospective buyers read the back before the flap. And that brings us to the power of testimonials. Clear and simple—testimonials work. So, today, begin to request testimonials from your customers or clients, business associates or anyone else whose positive comments about you or your business can be used to your advantage.

Ask them to send you a sentence of praise about you, the product or the service you represent. Accumulate the testimonials and build your own personal collection. Post them on your Web site, in your newsletters, in your power point presentations and on your promotional materials (such as flyers for a special event, postcards you may mail or press releases you send to the media). Carry copies with you so you can use them whenever you have a chance to acquire new clients or customers.

Testimonials speak for themselves; they are a powerful marketing tool that is better than anything you can say because it's other people who are heaping praise on you. Just think about it—if someone recommends a great restaurant, aren't you inclined to try it? And that's exactly what testimonials can do for you—encourage people to take a look at what you're selling or doing.

Call your best customers or business associates today and ask them to send you a testimonial. Also ask if you can use their name *and* ask them if they would be willing to send their testimonial to their friends as a recommendation of your product or service. Sometimes people are happy to give you a testimonial but aren't sure what to say. Here's how you can help them: Write a short testimonial yourself, send it to them and ask if what you wrote is an honest representation of how they feel (you probably know from previous comments what they like about your products or service). If they are okay with the comment, you can then use it attached with their name. But be sure *always to ask* if you can use a comment attributed to them.

Here's an example of a legitimate testimonial created from a client response to your product or service. Jane Doe tells you she absolutely loved your Relaxation Candle she purchased from you recently. You create the following testimonial and get her approval to use it: "I am using your Relaxation Candle every evening. I light it 10 minutes before bed, then I make my wish, blow out the candle and sleep like a baby. The aroma really works as a way to relax my busy mind." —Janie Doe, [Title], [City, State].

You'll earn respect and trust just by letting people tell the truth about how they feel about you and your product. Testimonials are one of the best and most inexpensive ways to promote your business, so get in the habit of writing down or recording the positive comments you hear and say: "May I quote you on that?"

Action: Ask people for testimonials and start using these comments in your promotional materials.

Chapter 27

Scrapbook Your Achievements.

Okay, okay … we know, scrapbooking may not be your thing. The thought of sitting around cutting and pasting stuff and oohing and ahhing over every cute little piece of bric-a-brac you find to jazz up the pages may leave you with one big fit of rolling eyes—but, there is something to be said for creating a scrapbook of your achievements. Why? Read on, my clever, nimble-fingered success story.

First of all, and you may find this hard to believe, but over time you will *forget*—yes, we said forget—some of the milestones of your career and your life. And that's not a bad thing because it means you're racking up so many accomplishments that the older ones get lost in the shuffle as your success grows. However, it's important that you have all of your accomplishments listed somewhere. And why not make it a scrapbook where you can include photographs of the people involved at the time, or personal notes written to you that highlight something you did or said that others appreciated?

You can even include newspaper articles that mention you, programs that list you as a guest presenter or really anything that helps to showcase every success you've enjoyed. This scrapbook is primarily for *your reference*—not something to bring out and ask people to flip through at your next dinner party or holiday gathering (if you think handing a friend a photo book of your children is in poor taste, try handing them your scrapbook!).

Make this scrapbook a professional journal (personal items—like your children's accomplishments—should go in another scrapbook). Keep it up-to-date and keep it handy. Put a picture of your compelling vision on the first page. That way you can refer to it at any moment to give yourself a dose of motivation and a kick in the pants to keep going.

Such a scrapbook also comes in handy when you need to provide someone with a concise list of your achievements. (For example, maybe you want to partner with a nonprofit on a special charity event and you totally forgot that you were the volunteer Chair of your son's preschool fundraising auction 10 years ago—and it was the most successful auction in the school's history!)

And finally—make this your personal brag book and have fun doing it. Doggone it, you've worked hard to reach your goals, and you should be able to relax with a cup of herbal tea and some lavender cookies and thumb through this personal tribute to remind yourself that you are empowered, beautiful and destined for greatness. This is your book and yes, this time *it's all about you!*

Action: Buy a new scrapbook and start bragging about *you!*

Chapter 28

Enroll in AU—Auto University.

Here's an idea that has been surrounding you for ages—and we bet you haven't even noticed. It's the concept of using your car as your own little mobile university. Cool, huh? Most of us spend a lot of time in the car. Even if it's just short jaunts here and there, the miles and the time accumulate. Why not put that time to good use by equipping your vehicle with CDs that provide information you can use—in building your business, in improving your self-confidence and in helping you learn how to get more enjoyment out of life.

We call it working toward getting your MBA—Massive Bank Account, that is.

It's easy to get started. Start compiling CDs that contain information you feel is valuable. Perhaps it's information about the ingredients contained in the product you sell. Or a motivational course designed to help you focus on your goals. Maybe it's an audio program on how to organize your life or instruction about how to practice the law of attraction.

Whatever learning programs you need or feel will be useful to your life and business, keep them in a CD case in your car so you can easily pop one into the player. (We strongly advise against listening to any CD that is designed to help you meditate or relax—you don't want to fall asleep at the wheel!) But having a stash of great music that lifts your spirits or helps you unwind is also a great idea. You may even want to keep some music handy that is especially energizing when you're feeling a little tired and are headed for an important meeting.

Remember—you are what you know and believe. If you keep learning and listening you're going to feel better about yourself and more empowered about the message you want to share with others. And the more you know the more you will grow. So find those CDs that are going to turn your car into your own mobile university and get started earning your Massive Bank Account degree!

Action: Get your wheels in motion and take advantage of every moment to learn something new.

Chapter 29

The Problem with Turkey and Dressing.

Most people have been given the task of cooking Thanksgiving dinner that includes roasting a turkey and preparing dressing. And chances are—if you've experienced this particular chore—the first time you attempted it, you were a little nervous. After all, this is a big bird and the main attraction for a major American holiday. (Why do you think so much has been written about the angst of families getting together for Thanksgiving dinner? It's because the person in charge of preparing the turkey has been reduced to a neurotic basket case by the time everyone arrives! So, duh … of course every dysfunctional seam in the family is going to split wide open.) Oh, not really … but it is a *big* responsibility.

The truth is, you may have called your mother or grandmother for advice (maybe more than once, right?), gotten out your favorite cookbook, consulted friends, and fretted and fussed until you were almost as done in as the poor bird itself. If you bought a frozen turkey, there is the whole business of when and how to thaw the thing (thaw it too late, and you're in big trouble and trust us—those rock hard suckers never thaw at the rate the instructions indicate).

If you're stuffing the bird, you can't stuff the thing the night before you cook it because that creates a health risk. And the whole business of stuffing (or dressing as people in the Midwest say) is another controversy. Uncle Fred likes cornbread stuffing, your picky cousin likes the store brand, your husband insists the seasoning be exactly like his mother's and well, it goes on and on (and if by chance you've never roasted a turkey and prepared dressing, please don't let our scenario scare you off!).

The point is, the first time may have been daunting but the next time was much easier, right? And that's how it is with starting a new business venture. You learn and you seek counsel and you dive in and . . . son of a gun, you may make a few mistakes but you will survive. The turkey was supposed to be done in three hours, but it took four hours, so you gave everyone another round of appetizers. Your presentation hit a snag when your computer crashed but you kept going, just talked from your heart and lo and behold, you still attracted some much needed venture capital.

The bottom line is this: Don't let initial jitters keep you from going forward. Realize that you will make mistakes and then learn from your mistakes. If you get really stuck, ask someone who's been there before for advice. Read a book that offers solutions. Pick apart the problem and put it in perspective, then solve it piece by piece.

It's okay to be a little nervous or even downright quaking in your to-die-for-suit you got such a bargain on at Nordstrom's big sale. But keep going and learning and soon *you* will be the one others come to for advice. Promise.

Action: Choose one thing you have been afraid to do and master it this week!

Chapter 30

Our Closing Argument. (Regarding Your Success)

Throughout this book we have given you ideas and specific actions for helping you build your business. Whether you're developing a part-time source of income or designing an entirely new career that is based on strong entrepreneurial skills, we hope these action items will offer motivation and techniques you can use throughout your business-building efforts—and throughout your life!

In closing, we'd like to leave you with some words of wisdom from three of our favorite authors and their books. As we've often said, you grow by learning. Just as a plant needs nutrients and water to thrive, you need proven techniques and new ways of thinking and "doing" to thrive as an entrepreneur and as an individual who is happy and confident in all that you do.

Be Willing to Let Go of Unwilling

Dr. Wayne Dyer is well-known as an author and motivation speaker. His specials on public television attract large audiences and inspire people to change damaging habits. Reading his book, *Excuses Begone! How to Change Lifelong, Self-Defeating Thinking Habits,* we had a light bulb moment. About halfway through the book is a chapter titled "Willingness." Dr. Dyer begins by reminding us that most of us say we are willing to do what it takes to achieve our dreams but, in reality, it is usually just lip service. That is, we only *say* we are willing. Unfortunately, most times than not, people are unwilling to do whatever it takes in order to achieve their dreams. The two light bulb questions Dr. Dyer asks are: "What are you reluctant to do to make your dreams and your desires become your reality?" and "Are you willing to shed all unwillingness?"

He then goes on to suggest that you create your own list of things you are unwilling to do in order to recreate the life you want. We know, that sounds confusing, but here is the next step: Make the list and then erase it. That's right—erase it; in place of those things you are unwilling to do, write down this powerful quote: *"There is nothing I am unwilling to do (as long as it is aligned with my Source) in order to bring my dreams into reality."*

If you think about your own situation (as we have ours), you'll probably realize that Dr. Dyer is exactly right. There are things you are unwilling to do to reach your goals. When you discard unwillingness from your life, your excuses are gone, and you become unstoppable. You must understand and act on the fact that you need to do whatever it takes to fulfill your dreams. Even if that means going to your day job and working your "passion" in the evening, or giving up a well-deserved vacation because you need to spend time turning your dream into reality. It could be risking your rainy-day fund to start your own business, enrolling in a class to learn better skills or even something as simple as giving up your favorite television show every evening so you can conduct evening appointments or man your store. The big question is: Are you willing to let go of the unwilling? Unwillingness can be a real albatross to carry around; it's time to free it so you can soar.

Action: Write the powerful affirming quote above several times, and post it in places where you will constantly see it—like the bathroom mirror, on your car dash or on your computer monitor.

Excuses Begone! How to Change Lifelong, Self-Defeating Thinking Habits by Dr. Wayne Dyer. Carlsbad, CA: Hay House, Inc., 2009.

It's True—Your Life … and Success … are Waiting!

Another book we refer to often is *Excuse Me, Your Life is Waiting—The Astonishing Power of Feelings* by Lynn Grabhorn. From her fun, energy-proving "Woo-Woo Wands" exercise to other nuggets of fascinating insights, you'll find yourself rethinking old ways and transforming negative thinking into positive thinking. Written with Grabhorn's engaging sense of humor and no-nonsense style, you'll be chuckling as you learn new ways to change your thinking. Unfortunately, Lynn Grabhorn died in 2004, but her book—and her valuable advice—live on.

One exercise we can't do without (nor should you!) isn't new, but it is worth taking the time to do. Grabhorn calls it "Writing a New Script." According to Grabhorn, writing a new script is merely making up a wonderful little daydream and embracing it emotionally. And in order for it to be effective you must "get into" this daydream with every ounce of your emotion.

Here's the drill: Create a present-time narration about your want, spoken out loud. You may also write it, but Grabhorn says writing is second choice. It must never be about what is *going* to happen … only about what *has* or is happening. As you repeat this story to yourself (as if you were telling a friend), you must *feel* the joy and fulfillment this story gives you.

Yes, you will feel like a nitwit at first, but practice telling your story to the dog or cat or pick up a celebrity magazine and recite it to the dreamy actor on the cover. What Grabhorn is saying is that by repeating and believing in positive situations, you change the vibration of your energy. And the law of attraction is all about bringing positive results into your life by *putting forth* positive energy.

Here's a sample story: "I am so excited by how well my book turned out. Sales are growing every day, and I'm receiving more and more requests to speak to groups. I used to be afraid to speak before a large audience, but now I love it. I keep meeting so many interesting people, and I now have a fantastic idea for another book that I can't wait to start writing."

Once you've created your new script, repeat it every day. When a negative thought pops into your head, immediately dismiss it and get back to your script. You can change your thinking, and you can change your life. (Here's a fun little exercise you can try to give the law of attraction a test: Next time you're headed someplace where parking is always an issue, tell yourself something like the following, *and do it with conviction:* "I found the perfect parking spot right away." Believe it as you say it and see what happens!).

Excuse Me, Your Life is Waiting—The Astonishing Power of Feelings by Lynn Grabhorn. Charlottesville, VA: Hampton Roads Publishing Company, Inc., 2000.

The Wisdom of Money

Our last book is *The Value of Money* by Susan McCarthy. We love this book because it helped us discover not only the value, but also the wisdom of money. McCarthy explains that money is the bridge between our values and our material world. And because of that, we needn't be afraid of making money, saving money or investing money because money is the instrument we use to cultivate the most important values we wish to exemplify. Sound familiar? Yep—it is the same type of thinking Wallace D. Wattles offers in his century-old book we mentioned at the beginning of this book: *The Science of Getting Rich.*

McCarthy expounds on this theory by saying: "We don't really think concretely about what we want or what we value, and we don't consciously put our money into the service of those desires. Too often we just roll along and make the simpler decisions or decisions others recommend, or we try to keep things the way they've always been. We resist the hard work of exploring ourselves and then figuring out ways to allow our money to express what we believe in."

According to McCarthy, money is really a tool for growth. And after living some decades, we can both attest to that! We believe that learning about the relationship between money and values can lead you toward a better life. As McCarthy goes on to say: "The legacy we leave through our money is as much a spiritual one as it is a material one." She believes that so much money will change hands over the next decades that each of us has an opportunity to enter a brave new money world filled with challenge and opportunity.

Now is the time for you to decide exactly what you want your money to say about you. Or, said another way by McCarthy: "Money is the mirror in which we glimpse our true selves."

We hope you will embrace the opportunity and the challenges that lie before you. Something—maybe it was the amazing results you experienced from the product you created or a burning desire to be your own boss—motivated you to try something new. To invest your time, energy and passion into a business that you believe can change your life. Now is the time to determine where you want to be (financially, physically and emotionally) in a year, five years, even ten years. Commit to earning the income you need and want. And remember that your wealth will enable you to enhance not just your own life but also the lives of every member of your family and the lives of many others you may never meet.

The Value of Money by Susan McCarthy. New York, New York: The Penguin Group, 2008.

In closing, we just want to remind you that your values and integrity must be the footings that hold you steady when challenges occur. And challenges *will* occur. You will get frustrated, and you will allow that insidious dream stealer called doubt to slip into your consciousness. You may be tempted to partner with someone who talks a great game but intuitively you know does not share your values. Listen to what your gut tells you about people and situations. In his fascinating book, *Blink—the Power of Thinking Without Thinking,* Malcom Gladwell says: "… there are moments, particularly in times of stress, when haste does not make waste, when our snap judgments and first impressions can offer a much better means of making sense of the world." So if it *feels* wrong, chances are it is. At least be willing to investigate the situation thoroughly before risking your reputation or your finances.

Is it possible to make an enormous amount of money as an independent business owner—an entrepreneur? Yes. Will *you?* That question must be answered by you and you alone. But we do know the only way you will truly enjoy your life and be proud of the rewards you gain is if you let your wealth be a reflection of you as an honest, hard working and compassionate person. Your journey as a successful entrepreneur can be exhilarating and filled with new relationships that not only help build your bank account but also broaden your mind, your heart and your knowledge.

We encourage you to be bold, never to let fear keep you from trying something new or to wonder if you truly deserve to live extraordinarily well. The answer is: Yes, you do. With integrity guiding your actions and a strong commitment to your goals, you are absolutely unstoppable. Got that?

Bonus Chapter

The Playbook for Doing It on Your Own.

The reality is, today anyone can be in business. Tools and technology are easily accessible. One person can do the job of three or four. You don't have to be miserable working an 80 hour week. You don't have to deplete your life savings or put your loved ones at risk. There are plenty of opportunities available that can align with your passion. Pick the right one. Don't be talked into doing something for which you have no love. And then, get going on the actions to move your business forward *today*. Don't spend a long time preparing for action—no months of getting ready (saddling up as we like to call it). It's okay to wing it a bit at first, but just get going.

Maybe the right size of your company is five people—maybe it's 45 people, or maybe it's just you and your laptop. Don't worry about how big you will get, worry about how big you can grow your business one day at a time. Anyone who is willing to start an independent business and has the spirit to pursue her or his dream has a lot to be proud of already.

And speaking of pride, don't forget to take a minute and recognize those supporting your efforts. That may be a family member or a good friend who is keeping the kids a couple of mornings a week to help you get things going. Saying thank-you means a lot—and throwing in a few pizza gift certificates for a hassle-free dinner says even more.

If you're working with others, they will be far more efficient if you respect the life they have outside your business. Packing your business with burn-the-midnight-oil types doesn't guarantee success. As a matter of fact, it doesn't even guarantee they will be proficient in what they do. Good people supporting your efforts will find ways to get it done if they know you know their life is important too.

Put some fun in your business. Maybe that means you let the skiers involved in your business work around the great powder on the nearby mountain. Celebrate birthdays, take the staff on a surprise "outing" when you've had a good month. If you make products, give your employees the chance to name them if that's appropriate. For example, if you bake and sell specialty cupcakes, let your employees give new cupcakes a dashing name. They'll have a lot more fun selling those cupcakes if they have their own creativity invested in them.

Don't be afraid to brainstorm with your employees. And for crying out loud—if Joanie the sales clerk comes up with a killer promotion idea for the holidays, make sure you recognize and applaud her contribution. There's nothing like a boss or owner who takes the credit for others' ideas to put a real damper on employee morale.

If you have an idea you are passionate about, see that there is a need for your product or service in the marketplace, and have the work ethic and determination to see it through, chances are you will be a success. But it won't come overnight and it won't come if you sit back and simply wish it to happen. Success takes work, following through when an opportunity presents itself, and a compassionate spirit. Most of all, it means believing in yourself. And maybe Walt Disney said it best: "If you can dream it, you can do it."

Action: Stop thinking and get into action—Start RIGHT and Start BIG *today!*

Actionable One-Liners to Fire Up Results.

Here are a few one-liner ideas to help you focus on your goals and business success. Listed in alphabetical order, you can use any of them at any time.

1. Admit it when you make a mistake and learn from it.

2. Analyze your business at the end of every month—you can't count on progress if you can't count what's been accomplished.

3. A vacation is a vacation. Turn off the phone and leave the laptop at home.

4. Be positive. Learn to nip negativity in the bud and replace it with something positive.

5. Be the man/woman you are, and stop preparing—act, time is money.

6. Call your best friend once a week and don't talk about your business.

7. Carry cash. A prosperity mind-set begins with actually having money regardless of how much it is.

8. Don't say you're tired, even when you are.

9. Don't talk so much. Take a breath, get to the point and move on.

10. Don't whine and complain. No one wants to hear what is not working.

11. Eat at home with the family—don't give up the family dinner for one more meeting.

12. Get rid of the word "just." I "just" have a little business or I "just" work my business part- time or "just" for fun.

13. Keep receipts for the taxman. One organized tax file holds the answer to lower taxes.

14. Make a gratitude list at least once a week; it will keep you going in the down times.

15. Order a two-sided business card. Use the extra space for a compelling one-liner.

16. Packaging sells. Market your product or service like you were in retail—drive value.

17. Pay your bills on time even though you're too busy.

18. People hear what they see—look the part.

19. Post a family dream board so everyone knows and supports your goals.

20. Recognize burnout before you're charred. Learn to delegate.

21. "Recognize" yourself every now and then just in case no one else is.

22. Remember the spouse and children of close business partners. Movie tickets are a great idea.

23. Save something from every check, even if it is only $25.

24. Stay out of other people's business—you have enough business of your own.

25. Stop saying "I'll never be able to afford this." You bring about what you think about.

26. Teach your children well.

27. Use technology to get to more people sooner. Learn what you need to know.

28. Your customers/clients are Kings and Queens. Find ways to appreciate them often.

Bibliography

Chouinard, Yvon. *Let My People Go Surfing: The Education of a Reluctant Businessman.* New York: The Penguin Press, 2005.

Dyer, Wayne. *Excuses Begone! How to Change Lifelong, Self-Defeating Thinking Habits.* Carlsbad, CA: Hay House, Inc., 2009.

Gladwell, Malcolm. *Blink—The Power of Thinking Without Thinking.* New York: Little, Brown and Company, 2005.

Grabhorn, Lynn. *Excuse Me, Your Life is Waiting—The Astonishing Power of Feelings.* Charlottesville, VA: Hampton Roads Publishing Company, Inc., 2000.

McCarthy, Susan. *The Value of Money.* New York: The Penguin Group, 2008.

O'Connors, Patricia T. *Woe Is I—The Grammarphobe's Guide to Better English in Plain English.* New York: Riverhead Books/ The Berkley Publishing Group. New York, 1996.

Wattles, Wallace D. (Edited by Ruth L. Miller). *The New Science of Getting Rich.* New York: Atria Books/Beyond Words Publishing, Inc., 2007.

Put pen to paper...**Short Term Goals**

Start RIGHT. Start BIG.

Put pen to paper...**Big Bodacious Dreams**

Put pen to paper...**Marketing Ideas**

Put pen to paper...Web References

Put pen to paper...**Key Business Contacts**

Start RIGHT. Start BIG.

Put pen to paper...**Your Personal, Positive Affirmations**

About the Authors

Charlene Schuster-Knox's desire to help entrepreneurs achieve their true potential is fueled by over 25 years' experience in corporate America. Charlene rose to the top of each position she held. Throughout her years as a corporate executive, she thrived in various management roles including serving as vice president and general manager for multimillion and billion-dollar companies.

Charlene was also named "World Sales Leader" during her tenure as an executive with a multibillion dollar corporation. As Charlene became an expert in the field of independent business ownership, colleagues and business owners began seeking her advice. This prompted her to start her own consulting firm in 2002. Often described as a creative thinker and problem solving strategist, Charlene has unique and creative ways of approaching her clients' desired outcomes so they end up with solid, measurable results—and have fun in the process. She has traveled around the country as a public speaker teaching people the limitless financial possibilities of the entrepreneurial lifestyle.

Charlene lectures nationwide on the power of personal potential and has also authored, *Relaxation Rocks©—30 Ways to Unwind at Home.*

Learn more about Charlene at *www.charknox.com.*

Angela E. Soper is an award-winning writer and film producer who has years of experience creating a wide range of marketing and media materials for corporations. She specializes in helping individuals and companies tell their unique "stories" so they will stand out in the marketplace. For nine years she served as the Creative Director/ Screenwriter for a billion-dollar nework marketing company.

As a freelance writer her work has appeared in *The Washington Post, People* magazine, *The Salt Lake Tribune,* and *Park City Magazine.* She is the coauthor of *Values Sell: Transforming Purpose into Profit through Creative Sales and Distribution Strategies,* one of a series of books produced by Social Venture Network to help advance the movement for social responsibility in business.

As a filmmaker she coproduced and cowrote Courthouse Girls of *Farmland,* a documentary that has won top audience awards at film festivals in Colorado and Rhode Island and has screened at festivals throughout the United States, in Canada and in Australia.

Learn more about Angela at *www.rangewriter.com.*